A WEEKEND WITH DIEGO RIVERA

A WEEKEND WITH
DIEGO RIVERA
by Barbara Braun

RIZZOLI
NEW YORK

Pinté mi retrato para la
bella y famosa artista Irene
Rich, y fué en la ciudad de
Santa Bárbara de
la California del Sur
durante el mes de Enero
del año de 1941
Diego Rivera

Hola! Welcome to Mexico! Come on up to my studio and have a look around. This is where I keep the things that are most dear to me. Sometimes I work here, painting portraits of ordinary people I see on the street or of my special friends. More often, you'll find me sitting high up on a scaffolding somewhere, sketching out my plan to cover a big wall with one of my murals. But this is our weekend together, so my feet will stay firmly planted on the ground. As far as I'm concerned, art is for the people; it should tell them something in pictures. In my work, I tell the story of my nation, Mexico—its history, its Revolution, its amazing Indian past, and its present-day popular traditions. So you see, I try to teach through my art. You surely have heard about me because I'm very famous. Here in my country, I am revered as one of *los tres grandes,* one of the three greatest painters ever, but throughout the rest of the world I am known simply as

Diego Rivera

Like many people in Mexico, I am part Indian, so naturally many of the stories I tell in paint reflect my Indian heritage. It's very important to me to feel this link with the ancient Indians. Their early civilizations existed in Mexico long before the Spaniards came. That's why they are called Pre-Columbian, because they were here before Columbus arrived—many hundreds of years before, in fact—and they had remarkable artists, architects, and scientists. I like to tell people that in the Pre-Columbian world everything in the life of the people was artistic, from the palaces, temples, and magnificent frescoes that astonish us today, to the most ordinary pottery, children's toys, and even grinding stones. I feel very close to my fellow Mexicans and I love to remind them and the rest of the world of our achievements. Let me show you how.

See that wall over there? Those shelves are crammed with little clay figurines, masks, and pots from the oldest Pre-Columbian civilizations. I collect the objects they made, and I sometimes include them in my paintings. Most people have heard of the Aztecs and the Mayas, but there were many other civilizations as well—from Veracruz, Western Mexico,

Oaxaca, and elsewhere. I especially like the objects from a site in the Valley of Mexico called Tlatilco. They are among the most ancient Pre-Columbian works known. Later, I'll show you where they came from. I am actually planning and designing a huge museum to house them so that Mexico and the rest of the world can see what my people have created.

Everything about Mexico is thrilling for an artist. For example, look at the giant puppets that are clustered over there by the window near my easel. I always like to have them around; I so much admire the way Indian artists have made them—out of papier-mâché fitted on clay molds and wooden frames, painted with bright colors, to be taken out on special fiesta days. Some of the best ones are called *calaveras.* These represent skeletal figures that perform dances on the Day of the Dead, an important holiday that is celebrated all over Mexico in November. You may think they look scary, but people here don't; in fact, we think they are comical. They remind us that life and death are always intertwined—that winter is always followed by spring. On November 2 children all over Mexico eat sugar skulls decorated with candy.

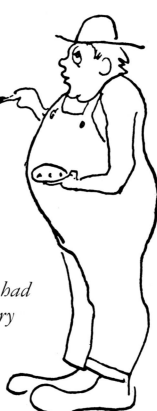

Rivera made many self-portraits. He was oafish and funny looking, but he had great personal warmth. A huge man with an enormous appetite for life, he was witty and charming and had amazing vitality. Although you might not think so, he was very attractive to women.

Here is a mural Rivera painted of the Day of the Dead ceremony in Mexico City. There is a self-portrait of the artist here—can you find it? This painting in the Ministry of Public Education shows how closely he identified with the Mexican people. One of the dancing calaveras on the stage is dressed like a peasant in overalls and a straw hat called a sombrero. This is the way Rivera usually dressed.

Rivera drew this sleeping woman during his trip to Italy. Seen from below, simple and monumental, she is like a figure in a fresco on a wall.

As you can see, I am a large man. My friends say that I'm larger than life. I'm not exactly a beauty, I know. In fact, my wife, Frida, calls me "the toad," and you can see why. There has always been something unusual about me. I was singled out for my talent in drawing when I was very young. When I was six years old, my family moved from Guanajuato, where I was born, to Mexico City. Before long I got a scholarship to study at the Academy of Fine Arts of San Carlos. My teachers encouraged me and awarded me a state scholarship to study in Europe where I would be exposed to the old masters in the great museums, churches, and palaces, as well as to exciting new artistic activity, first in Spain and then in Paris. I only planned to stay for four years—I stayed for fourteen instead.

In Paris I made friends with Picasso and many other artists, including Amedeo Modigliani, Piet Mondrian, and Robert Delaunay, who were changing the whole idea of what art was. I made many cubist pictures in which the subject was painted as a series of small triangles, cubes, and rectangles. Even then, my canvases told stories. Not only that, they were clearer and more colorful than Picasso's! I was also in touch with fellow Mexicans studying abroad, especially my good friend, David Alfaro Siqueiros. While we were in Paris, Mexico was struggling to find itself after years of civil war and social unrest. Although we were enjoying ourselves in Europe and learning all about the latest tendencies in art, we were always thinking of home and listening to news about Mexico. Finally, in 1920, we decided that our country needed us and that we should return to help create a new art for a new nation. It was our hope that the wealth held by the European minority could be shared more fairly with the Indians and *mestizos*—that is, people with mixed Indian and European ancestry—so that the vast majority would have a chance to lead a better life. We felt strongly that a good basis for this new art would be a return to our Pre-Columbian roots.

The many sketches Rivera made in the isthmus of Tehuantepec became the basis of this painting depicting Tehuantepec dancers. A version of a fresco in the Ministry of Public Education, it captures the lush vegetation and brilliant colors of the tropical lowlands.

Rivera's cubist painting, Zapatista Landscape (The Guerrilla), *shows his early interest in Mexican subject matter. It contains references to the* sarape *(shawl), rifle, and* sombrero *that are associated with the Indian peasant revolutionary, Emiliano Zapata, as well as to the Mexican landscape. Before he returned to Mexico, Rivera made a special trip to Italy to study Etruscan, Byzantine, and Renaissance art, and especially to learn how Renaissance artists revived their native Italian classical heritage in fresco painting.*

When we returned home in 1921 we jumped right into the great cultural renewal that the new government was sponsoring. Called the Mexican Renaissance, its aim was to revive the native political and artistic traditions that had been denied by four hundred years of European rule. As painters, we were encouraged to create murals in public buildings so that ordinary people could be aware and proud of their heritage and culture, which Europeans had frowned upon. We wanted to enlist their support for the enormous task of rebuilding Mexican society.

The big three muralists—Siqueiros, Jose Clemente Orozco, and myself, of course—as well as many others considered ourselves to be ordinary workers and craftsmen, so we formed a union of artists and artisans, together with masons, carpenters, and plasterers. And we decided that, in order to make our message clear to everyone, even those who couldn't read, we would paint recognizable pictures rather than the abstract paintings that some of us had done in Paris.

My first important assignment was to decorate the walls of the Ministry of Public Education in Mexico City. To prepare myself, I went on government-sponsored trips to the Yucatán peninsula and the isthmus of Tehuantepec. I studied the ruins of Pre-Columbian cities and visited Indian villages whose inhabitants were famous for their colorful customs and clothing. I especially admired the beautiful Tehuantepec women, stately in their long dresses and braided hairdos, so like their Pre-Columbian ancestors. When I felt as though I had absorbed enough, I portrayed Mexican life and culture in all its variety—its regions, landscapes, industries, celebrations, and struggles.

Several frescoes in the Ministry of Public Education focus on Mexican laborers. Leaving the Mine, *opposite, depicts one of the major industries of Mexico's western highlands—mining. By showing the physical effort involved in climbing out of the mine, Rivera portrays the difficult conditions and hard life of Mexican miners.*

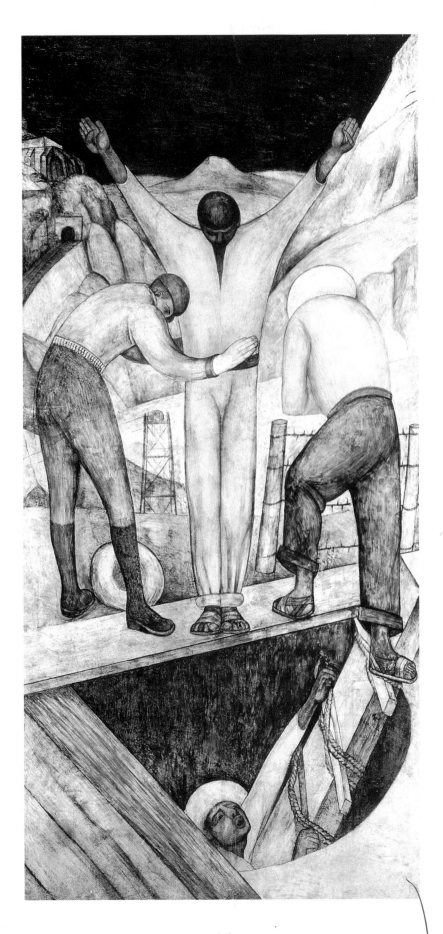

As time went on, I became more interested in telling the story of the Mexican Revolution—its heroes, songs, enemies, battles, and victories. I wanted to encourage people to further action. That's when I met the talented and pretty young art student, Frida Kahlo, who soon became my wife. You may have heard of her—she also became a great painter. Frida came to watch me paint every day and brought me lunch, which I would sometimes eat on the scaffolding because I didn't want to interrupt my work. You can see her portrait in this panel on the upper story of the Ministry of Education; I showed her handing out guns to soldiers prepared to defend the Revolution.

This photograph of Diego Rivera and Frida Kahlo, taken around 1940, reveals what an odd couple the two artists made. Their relationship was a stormy one, but they remained devoted to one another for the rest of their lives.

A good example of Teotihuacán fresco painting, dated 400–600 A.D., this scene represents a Pre-Columbian goddess providing the water needed to make plants grow. Below, small figures dance and sing happily.

To create the big murals, I would first do a full-size preparatory drawing (called a cartoon) and sketch it on the wall. Then my assistants would help me mix paint and fill in parts of the mural under my instruction. This technique, called fresco, is a complicated one. It involves painting on fresh, wet plaster and has to be done quickly before the plaster dries and becomes part of the wall. Although this process had been used all over Europe for many centuries, I was also aware of mural paintings in the great Pre-Columbian city of Teotihuacán, just 30 miles north of Mexico City, and in the Mayan area at Bonampak. In fact, I decided to try what I thought was an ancient Mexican technique of mixing the pigments with cactus juice, but when it didn't work I returned to traditional European methods.

All in all I painted 235 panels covering a total area of fifteen thousand square feet in just one building. That's an amazing accomplishment, you'll have to agree! And mainly I did it all by myself! What's more, I never once doubted that I was up to the task. It makes me hungry just thinking about it! Let's go around the corner and get some enchiladas.

After completing that project I became the leading painter in the land. My next big project was in the new agricultural college at Chapingo, where I covered the chapel with brilliantly colored frescoes. Here, I took as subject matter the message of our great revolutionary hero, Zapata. By comparing growth in nature to growth in society, I illustrated his point that Mexican peasants need to have their own land to plant their crops. This way, they can have control of their lives. Many people say that the chapel is my finest achievement, and perhaps they're right. I can't deny that these murals are knock-outs. Oh, to be young again, and to believe that everything is possible! But now let me show you my murals in the National Palace.

The curving, sensuous forms and bright palette of the Chapingo murals owe a great deal to French Symbolists like Paul Gauguin. The muscular figures that seem to emerge from compartments on the ceiling recall those of Michelangelo. The conception of the murals is based on the Aztec notion of the creation of life through death and destruction. The end result is an overpowering expression of the artist's fervent belief in the ideals of the reborn nation.

The entryway announces the theme of renewal—the shrouded corpses of the revolutionary heroes, Zapata and Otilio Mantano, are buried beneath a fruitful cornfield.

Here we are! In 1929 I began work on my great and sweeping history of the Mexican nation, painted on the walls of the National Palace's main stairway. This building, erected on the site of the Aztec emperor Moctezuma's palace, houses the offices of the Mexican president and the federal government. Was I ever ambitious with this one! It took me six years to complete! I wanted to show all the Mexican people who come here what I imagine our great country looked and felt like throughout the ages. So I painted this huge panorama, sort of like a

movie sequence, of all the important events, people, and myths that make up our magnificent history, from Pre-Columbian to modern times. Fortunately, I have a remarkable ability to visualize and sketch a complicated and highly detailed work and fit it into an architectural space in no time flat. Otherwise, this fresco probably still wouldn't be finished!

To picture the modern period Rivera could refer to photographs or engravings, but for the Pre-Columbian world no such evidence existed. To help him imagine this ancient world he turned to the handful of Indian illustrated manuscripts (called codices) and old Spanish records (called chronicles) that have survived from the period after the conquest of Mexico.

Rivera modeled this battle scene fresco at the Palace of Cortés in Cuernavaca after the 16th-century drawing of ritual Aztec combat you see below.

I began my giant composition on the right-hand wall with a vision of the myths of the Pre-Columbian epoch, centering on the great Mexican hero, Quetzalcoatl (also a god in the form of a feathered serpent). He taught his followers the arts and crafts of civilization—maize cultivation, stone carving, weaving, ceramics, painting, music, and dance. In the central section (on page 27) I continued the history of ancient Mexico with a representation of the Spanish conquest of the Aztec capital, Tenochtitlán. See there, at the exact center of the composition? That's where I placed the emblem of the Aztec state, an eagle on a cactus with a serpent in its mouth. Aztec myth says that the tribe wandered through the desert until such an eagle appeared to announce their new home.

Rivera used this illustration from the Codex Tovar as a model for the centerpiece of the National Palace mural, opposite.

The same year that I began the murals at the National Palace, I was commissioned by the American ambassador Dwight Morrow to execute a mural as a gift from the United States to Mexico. It was to be in Cuernavaca at the colonial palace of Hernan Cortés, who conquered Mexico in 1521. Here I depicted a crucial battle between Cortés, with his Indian allies from Tlaxcala and Texcoco, and the Aztecs who ruled Cuernavaca. This battle took

place immediately before the Spanish conquest of Tenochtitlán, so I painted the National Palace's staircase mural and the one in Cuernavaca at the same time, traveling back and forth between the two sites. I used the same source material for both. Now you know one of the secrets which enable me to paint so much so swiftly!

I wanted to show what it must have been like when heroic Aztec warriors, dressed as eagle and jaguar knights, carrying weapons of wood and stone, elaborate shields, and battle standards, fought against the Spanish soldiers of Cortés with their steel armor, swords, and horses. The Indians had never seen horses before and found them terrifying. I also painted a portrait of our great hero Zapata with his noble white horse to show the continuing tradition of great Mexican warriors. Although I had more work than I could handle painting these murals in Mexico City and Cuernavaca, I accepted still more work illustrating books. It was a relief to work small with just brush and ink for a change!

Rivera's brush line could be gentle or forceful, depending on his subject. His illustrations for an English translation of the Popol Vuh, *the sacred book of the Quiche Maya, above, focus on the story of hero twins who play ball against the lords of the underworld.*

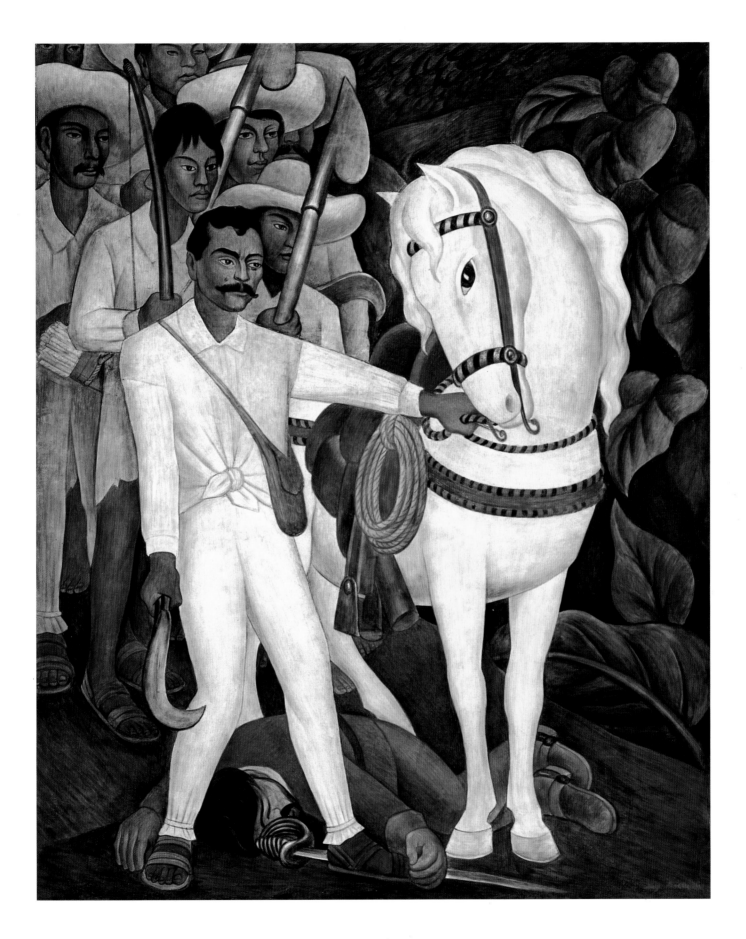

Rivera modeled the tall spindles in his mural, Detroit Industry, *below right, after these giant, blocky Toltec figures atop a pyramid at the ancient site of Tula.*

Rivera's murals of the construction of automobile engines and the operation of blast furnaces, foundries, and conveyor belts suggest that these machines are modern-day versions of Pre-Columbian gods. These murals reveal that Rivera never forgot the cubist idea of capturing the speed and intensity of modern life.

By now my fame had spread to the United States and many people asked me to paint murals there. This was a good time to accept their offers since the government had changed in Mexico and the new president didn't want to spend money on more murals. So I left Mexico in 1930, along with my colleagues Orozco and Siqueiros. I stayed in the United States for nearly four years. During that time, I was happy to spread the word about the greatness of Mexico, and I was keen to get a good look at the American industrial know-how that my country needed so badly. I now realized that technology, rather than armed battle, was the best means of organizing a new society. So when Henry Ford commissioned a mural celebrating automobile production in the Detroit Institute of Arts, I jumped at the opportunity. I spent many days in Ford's River Rouge plant studying the auto assembly line, the first of its kind in the world. I was impressed with the power and speed of those machines and the way the workers so rhythmically fit in! It reminded me of the way I imagine ancient Mexican farmers worked in harmony with nature and the seasons.

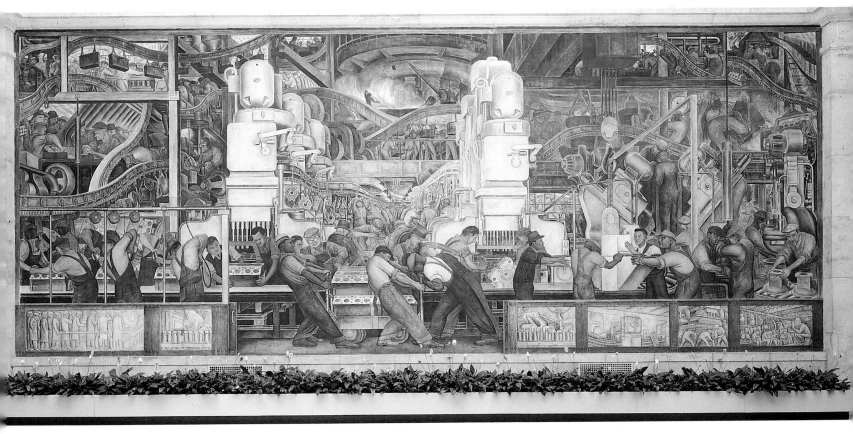

After the big controversy over my mural in the RCA Building in New York, when my patron Nelson Rockefeller destroyed the mural after I refused to make a change in it, I decided to return to my beloved Mexico. I was so glad to be home again, where I could express myself freely and conduct my life as I pleased. Besides, lots of famous people from all over—the United States, Latin America, Europe, even Russia—came to visit me and see my work, so I really didn't need to travel anymore.

Come with me now and I'll show you what I love to do best. I walk around observing and sketching in the city and country, always with sketchbooks of different sizes tucked into my pockets. I return over and over to my favorite places, setting down my impressions in pen, pencil, and charcoal. I've always been good at drawing. If I'm attracted to a face or figure or scene I sketch it lightly, then repeat the image in greater detail, and then finally I develop it into a larger finished drawing or put it into an oil painting or fresco. Let me show you some of the people and places that inspire my work.

Almost anything having to do with the daily life and customs of Mexico fascinates and touches me: the markets in Indian villages with their colorful piles of fruits, vegetables, and woven goods, as well as the crowds, the activity, and the little dogs running about. I'm moved by the simple dignity of Indian women in their shawls and long skirts sitting cross-legged on the ground, tenderly caring for their young children or selling their wares. One of the scenes I never tire of is Xochimilco, a southern suburb of Mexico City where flowers are raised on little artificial mud islands called floating gardens. People boat in the canals, and everywhere there are Indian women carrying, arranging, and selling enormous bouquets of beautiful flowers. Did you know that flowers always adorn even the humblest Indian hut, and that the Aztecs worshiped a goddess of flowers?

Rivera's many paintings of Indian women selling flowers, like Flower Day *on page 33, were often based on Aztec statues of flower and fertility goddesses, echoing their compact bodies, kneeling postures, and braided hairdos.*

Buenas dias! It's Sunday. Come with me to one of my favorite haunts: the Alameda Park in downtown Mexico City. Here, people stroll in stylish outfits, as I did when I was a boy, and many important historical events have taken place. I very much value the idea of public parks where people can relax with their families and friends on Sundays after working hard all week. This is why I was happy to accept a commission to adorn a great waterworks in Chapultepec, the biggest, most beautiful and historically important park in all of Mexico. I painted murals in the pumping station on the theme of life-giving water. Quite appropriate for a waterworks, don't you think? Then, since this waterworks was built on the site of a sacred Aztec shrine and springs, I also designed a huge mosaic fountain outside the pumping station depicting the Aztec rain god Tlaloc, who is associated with flowing water.

I am keenly interested in Mexican antiquities, and whenever I get the chance I collect them as a way of honoring and preserving ancient Mexican artistic achievements. I feel they are equal or superior to the art produced by other ancient civilizations like Egypt, Mesopotamia, and Cambodia. There are a lot of archaeological investigations going on all over Mexico. A fascinating, very early site called Tlatilco was recently discovered in a brickworks in Mexico City. I go there every chance I get to see what buried treasures have been unearthed. Everybody there knows how interested I am in these objects and they bring them to me. That's how I accumulated so many hundreds of them. My wife Frida often accuses me of spending all my money on them so that there is nothing left to pay the bills. Some of my artist friends also collect these objects, and sometimes we swap them.

As I said earlier, I have decided to give all of my Pre-Columbian treasures to my fellow countrymen so that they will possess their great artistic heritage forever. The special museum I have designed to house them is modeled after ancient Mexican and Mayan buildings. I call it Anahuacalli. In the Aztec language that means "house of the Valley of Mexico."

Rivera designed a studio for himself in Anahuacalli adorned with his beloved calaveras *and Judas figures, as well as cartoons for some of his murals and his favorite Pre-Columbian objects. Unfortunately, he was never able to use it, because he died soon after it was completed.*

In the Hotel del Prado mural, Rivera pictured himself as a boy of the late 19th century, holding the hand of a female calavera who represents both his mother and the Mexican spirit. Behind him is a portrait of Frida Kahlo, and on either side is an assemblage of historical characters and events.

Another project that has occupied me on and off for many years is the decoration of the walls of the patio corridor of the National Palace, near the stairway fresco I did some time ago. Here I want to show all the visitors to this great building the fabulous daily life and customs of our ancient ancestors. The first and largest fresco panel (on pages 44–45) depicts the great marketplace of the Aztec capital, Tenochtitlán. People traveled here from all the distant regions of Mexico, bringing their foodstuffs, herbal medicines, ceramics, featherworks, precious gold and mosaic ornaments, and woven garments as tribute to the Aztec emperor.

I tried to imagine what it must have been like by drawing on the accounts of Cortés and other eyewitnesses at the time of the Spanish Conquest. In the center of my composition I placed a royal steward wearing the turquoise crown of the Aztec nobility, carrying an elegant feather fan. He oversees the rich array of goods that are laid out for sale or barter by the many colorfully dressed merchants. I took their costumes from codex illustrations and based some of the incidents and curiosities in this bustling scene on Pre-Columbian art. For example, a little flower girl pulls a wheeled ceramic toy like those found in Veracruz sites. Can you find it? Below the main scene I painted several small panels depicting the human labor that produces the goods at the market—raising and harvesting crops, weaving, preparing food, and counting tribute to the emperor. Four other fresco panels on the patio corridor walls portray the arts and industries of the regional cultures that contributed their products to the Aztec market. A sixth panel depicts Cortés landing in Mexico, and I have plans for others. I just hope I have time to finish them.

Small ceramic figures with wheels such as this one representing a jaguar have been found among Veracruz ruins on the Gulf Coast of Mexico. They date from about A.D. 300–900 and were made as children's toys. The wheel was never used for practical purposes in ancient Mexico, but appears in a few figurines, like this toy. Rivera incorporated a jaguar figurine like this one in his painting of the Aztec capital's market, The Great City of Tenochtitlán.

Just to the right of the jaguar figurine in Rivera's mural are two burden bearers, common sights in ancient and modern-day Indian markets. Since no wheeled transportation existed and no animals were used for carting, people carried goods on their backs, often over great distances. For Rivera this image captured the essence of the ordinary Mexican people he loved. He modeled the bearers after this terra-cotta figure from his own collection of Pre-Columbian art. The figure is from western Mexico and was made between 250 B.C. and A.D. 250.

45

All my life there has been so much to accomplish and so little time. . . . But now I must get back to work. I've enjoyed our visit and hope I have shown you how important it is to search for your roots and celebrate your heritage, as I have always done. *Adios amigo!*

WHERE TO SEE RIVERA

No book can do justice to the monumentality and grandeur of Rivera's murals in their architectural settings. Most of these are in Mexico City, but there are also a number in the United States.

Fortunately, if you can't get to see the murals, you can find Rivera's fresco panel and easel painting versions of them in many public collections in the United States and Mexico, which also include many of his smaller paintings and drawings.

The following is a selected list of the locations of Rivera's murals and smaller works.

UNITED STATES

CALIFORNIA

San Francisco was Rivera's first stop during his stay in the United States in the early 1930s and he had many patrons there, so the city is especially rich with his work.

Rivera painted the mural at City College of San Francisco, *Pan-American Unity (Marriage of the Artistic Expression of the North and South of this Continent),* his largest mural in the United States, for the Golden Gate International Exposition of 1939–40. He intended it to promote good will between the United States and Mexico at a fearful time when World War II was beginning in Europe.

The mural in the San Francisco Art Institute's exhibition hall, *The Making of a Fresco, Showing the Building of a City* (page 5), shows the design and construction of a modern industrial city. The activities of the workers and planners are seen through a painted scaffolding that supports a fresco artist, Rivera himself, and his assistants.

The San Francisco Museum of Modern Art owns the important oil paintings *The Flower Carrier* (page 48) and *Symbolic Landscape,* as well as many drawings and figure studies for various frescoes Rivera painted in the city.

The M.H. de Young Museum hosted one of Rivera's first retrospectives in 1939. The museum owns some pencil and charcoal drawings and the painting *Two Women and a Child*.

In Southern California, you can stop by the Los Angeles County Museum of Art to see *Flower Day* (page 33) and a few small works, including pencil, charcoal, and pen-and-ink drawings. In San Diego, the San Diego Museum of Art owns *A Lady in White* and a *Self-Portrait*.

ILLINOIS

At the Art Institute of Chicago you can see *Portrait of Madame Marcoussis* and some of Rivera's drawings.

MASSACHUSETTS

The Fogg Art Museum at Harvard University in Cambridge owns a few pencil drawings, including *Sleeping Woman* (page 10).

The Smith College Museum of Art in Northampton owns the *Self-Portrait* on page 4, as well as *Market Scene,* a large, movable fresco.

MICHIGAN

The Detroit Institute of Arts has one of Rivera's greatest murals, *Detroit Industry* (page 31), depicting the industrial process at the Ford Motor Company plant in River Rouge, Michigan. Twenty-seven panels are arranged around an interior court in the main section of the museum. The Institute also has a number of his smaller works, including *Portrait of Edsel Ford, Portrait of Robert Tannahill,* some pencil and charcoal drawings and watercolors, and cartoons for various panels of *Detroit Industry.*

MINNESOTA

Rivera's distinctive *Portrait of the Knight Family* is at the Minneapolis Institute of Arts.

NEW YORK

For his one-person show at the The Museum of Modern Art in 1931, Rivera made several large, movable fresco panels, including *Agrarian Leader Zapata* (page 29), which is still in its collection. MoMA also owns several watercolors and pencil and charcoal drawings, including a study for the fresco *Day of the Dead in the Country,* in the Ministry of Public Education, and other studies for frescoes, such as the destroyed Rockefeller Center mural. It also owns five watercolors from Rivera's notebook, "May Day, Moscow," which he painted in Russia in 1928.

You can see Rivera's painting *Copalli* at the Brooklyn Museum.

PENNSYLVANIA

The Philadelphia Museum of Art has one of the largest collections of the master's work in the United States. It contains *Liberation of the Peon* and *Sugar Cane,* both large movable frescoes; several pencil studies for frescoes at the Ministry of Public Education in Mexico City, the chapel at Chapingo, and other frescoes in Mexico City and Cuernavaca; as well as important works in charcoal and brush and ink.

TEXAS

The Cubist *Still Life with Gray Bowl* is at the Lyndon Baines Johnson Library and Museum in Austin.

MEXICO

Mexico City

A great number of Rivera's murals and paintings can be found in Mexico City.

Diego Rivera painted his first mural, *Creation,* in the auditorium at the National Preparatory School in 1922 and 1923. It is a composition of symbolic figures and natural elements resembling Italian Renaissance frescoes of religious subjects.

The murals at the Ministry of Public Education, painted between 1923 and 1928, contain 116 major fresco compositions and many secondary panels representing Rivera's vision of the entire modern Mexican world. Be sure to reserve a good block of time if you want to see all the murals in this building. In the Court of Fiestas you will find the frescoes depicting the Day of the Dead celebration on the ground floor (page 9), and on the third floor, the panel titled *Distributing Arms* (page 16), which contains a portrait of Rivera's wife Frida Kahlo.

At the National Palace, a grand structure on Mexico City's vast main plaza, Rivera's murals occupy two adjacent areas in the center of the building. Their subject is the history of Mexico from Pre-Columbian to modern times. The frescoes are organized in two parts: *From the Conquest to the Future* on the wall of the great stairway leading from the ground floor to the second story, and *From the Pre-Hispanic Civilization to the Conquest* on the corridor walls of the Palace's main patio.

The mural at the Palace of Fine Arts, titled *Man, Controller of the Universe,* is a copy by Rivera of a fresco he originally painted at Rockefeller Center in New York, which was destroyed. A figure of a worker in overalls at the controls of a huge machine dominates the composition.

The Diego Rivera Mural Museum houses the Hotel del Prado mural (the hotel was damaged by an earthquake in 1985). *Dream of a Sunday Afternoon in the Alameda* (pages 40–41) presents a summary of Mexican history and the artist's personal role in it. The long line of figures, with Rivera as a boy in the center, appears to promenade in the Alameda Park.

The National Museum of Art contains many of Rivera's early canvases from his years in Europe, such as *Nôtre Dame de Paris, Breton Girl, Portrait of Adolfo Best Maugard,* and the important *Zapatista Landscape (the Guerrilla)* (page 13), as well as watercolor illustrations for books.

At the Museum of Modern Art you'll find *The Grinder* and several paintings from late in his life, including *Portrait of Lupe Marin, Day of the Dead, Nocturnal Landscape,* and *The Temptations of St. Anthony.*

The Hospital de la Raza houses Rivera's mural *The History of Medicine: The People's Demand for Better Health.* Located in the entrance foyer, it is a celebration of Pre-Columbian and modern medicine.

The Lerma Waterworks project, created in 1951, consists of two parts: frescoes depicting the importance of water to humankind on the floor and walls of a great water tank inside a pavilion, and a giant mosaic sculpture representing the Aztec rain god, Tlaloc, in an outdoor fountain (pages 36–37). Unfortunately, the frescoes in the water tank have been badly eroded by forty years of rushing water.

On the front of the Theater of the Insurgents, a movie theater on one of Mexico's busiest avenues, Rivera's giant mosaic mural presents *A Popular History of Mexico* from Pre-Columbian to modern times, with special attention to dance and drama. It was made in 1953.

Rivera designed and built the pyramid-shaped Anahuacalli (The Diego Rivera Museum) to house his vast collection of Pre-Columbian artifacts, and to serve as his studio and, eventually, his tomb. Here you'll find hundreds of Pre-Columbian figurines, as well as some paintings and cartoons by Rivera.

Chapingo

The former chapel of the university administration building at the Autonomous University of Chapingo (once a convent) contains what may be Rivera's masterpiece. Painted in 1926–27, these murals on the theme of natural evolution and social revolution were intended to provide inspiration for a new generation of Mexican agricultural workers (pages 20–21).

Cuernavaca

Murals cover three walls of an outdoor, second-floor patio of the 16th-century Palace of Cortés. Their subject is the history of Cuernavaca and Morelos, from the Spanish Conquest in 1521 to the agrarian revolt led by Emiliano Zapata in 1911.

Guanajuato

Rivera's birthplace, now the Diego Rivera Museum, contains a number of his early canvases, including *Sailor at Lunch,* and *Bather of Tehuantepec.* It is also rich with watercolors, including illustrations for a translation of the *Popol Vuh,* a sacred text of the Quiche Maya, and pencil, charcoal, and brush-and-ink drawings.

IMPORTANT DATES IN RIVERA'S LIFE

1886   Diego Rivera is born on December 13 in Guanajuato, Mexico.

1889   Rivera begins to draw.

1896   Rivera enters an evening art course at the Academy of San Carlos in Mexico City, where his family moved in 1892.

1898–
1905   Rivera enrolls in regular classes at San Carlos when he is awarded a scholarship. He perfects his technique, studying perspective, figure drawing, and landscape painting. In 1905 he receives a government pension.

1906   Rivera receives a modest scholarship to study in Europe. He exhibits fifteen of his works at San Carlos. He joins *Savia Moderna,* a pro-modernist group of young artists, architects, and intellectuals.

1907–
1908   Rivera studies in Spain under the realist painter Eduardo Chicharro y Aguera and copies masterworks in the Prado Museum, including paintings by Goya, El Greco, and Velázquez. He becomes friendly with leading avant-garde artists in Madrid.

1909–
1910   Rivera lives in Paris in the Latin Quarter and studies at the Louvre and various academies. He exhibits his work at the Society of Independent Artists. He also visits Bruges, London, Brittany, and Madrid, and in October 1910 returns to Mexico, where he has a successful show of his European work. The Mexican Revolution begins.

1911–
1912   Rivera returns to Paris in June 1911 and befriends Amedeo Modigliani. He is influenced by the Cubism of his neighbor, the Dutch painter Piet Mondrian, and exhibits paintings at the Society of

Independent Artists and the Autumn Salon. He travels, paints, and exhibits in Toledo, Spain.

1913–
1917

Rivera paints in the cubist style in Paris and Spain. He becomes very friendly with leading Parisian modernists such as Fernand Léger, Marc Chagall, and Jacques Lipchitz, and he meets Juan Gris and Pablo Picasso. His first one-person show in Paris is a great success, and he also exhibits in group shows in various European capitals and in New York. In 1917 he breaks with some of his Cubist friends and begins to return to a realistic style based mainly on his study of Cézanne.

1920–
1921

Rivera travels to Italy to study Etruscan, Byzantine, and Renaissance art in preparation for his return to Mexico to paint murals in the service of the Revolution. Rivera returns to Mexico in July 1921 and is immediately appointed to art-related government positions. He travels to Yucatán to see Pre-Columbian sites.

1922

Rivera paints his first mural in the National Preparatory School in Mexico City. In June he marries Guadalupe Marín. In the fall he and other muralists form the Union of Technical Workers, Painters, and Sculptors.

1923–
1927

Rivera paints the walls of the Ministry of Public Education, often working eighteen hour days, for four years. He earns very little from his frescoes, so increasingly he supports himself through the sale of oil paintings, watercolors, and drawings, often to American patrons.

1926

Rivera begins his murals in the chapel of the National Agricultural School in Chapingo while continuing to work on the Ministry of Education murals.

1927

Rivera's marriage breaks up. He travels to the Soviet Union in September and remains there until June 1928, when he returns to Mexico.

1929   Rivera is appointed director of the Academy of San Carlos, but is forced to resign in 1930. He begins work on the stairway murals of the National Palace and marries Frida Kahlo. U.S. Ambassador to Mexico Dwight Morrow commissions Rivera to paint a mural at the Palace of Cortés in Cuernavaca.

1930–
1934   Rivera accepts commissions to paint murals in the United States in San Francisco, Detroit, and New York. He is given retrospective exhibitions in San Francisco and New York. Wherever he goes in the United States, Rivera creates controversies, attracts admirers, and leaves a lasting impression on painters who emulate his mural techniques. In January 1934 Rivera returns to Mexico and resumes work on the stairway mural at the National Palace.

1937–   Rivera receives no commissions to paint public walls in Mexico. However, he does paint a mural for the 1939 Golden Gate Exposition in San Francisco. In 1942 Rivera returns to the National Palace and begins a series of panels on Pre-Columbian cultures for the second-floor courtyard. Construction begins on Anahuacalli, the museum he designed to house his vast collection of Pre-Columbian art.

1943   Rivera undertakes two new mural projects in Mexico City. He begins to receive major honors in Mexico.

1947   Rivera is hospitalized with pneumonia in March. He begins a mural in the new Hotel del Prado, which he completes the following year.

1949   The first major retrospective of Rivera's work is held at the Palace of Fine Arts in Mexico City. It includes over one thousand works and is inaugurated by the President of Mexico, Miguel Aleman, who calls him "a national treasure."

1950   Rivera's paintings, along with those of José Clemente Orozco, David Alfaro Siqueiros, and Rufino Tamayo, are exhibited in the Mexican pavilion at the Venice Biennale. The Mexican government awards Rivera the National Art Prize.

1951   Rivera completes the pre-Conquest series of murals at the National Palace.

1953   Rivera works on two murals in Mexico City: a large mosaic at the new Theater of the Insurgents, and a fresco for the Hospital de la Raza which will be his last fresco commission.

1954   Frida Kahlo dies.

1955   Rivera is diagnosed with cancer but continues to work, creating many easel paintings, primarily portraits. He marries Emma Hurtado, his art dealer since 1946. He gives the building and collections of Anahuacalli in trust to the Mexican people. He travels to Moscow, where he receives treatment for his cancer.

1956   Rivera leaves Moscow and travels throughout Eastern Europe, sketching and painting. In April he returns to Mexico and continues to work. On December 8, the nation pays tribute to him on his seventieth birthday.

1957   Rivera dies of heart failure in his San Angel studio. He is officially honored and buried in the Rotunda of Illustrious Men in Mexico City.

LIST OF ILLUSTRATIONS

The following is a list of the titles and locations for works of art reproduced in this book. Dimensions are given in both inches or feet and centimeters or meters, first by height, then by width.

Page 3
Rivera in front of unfinished mural in Cuernavaca, 1930. Photo courtesy Sophia Smith Archives, Smith College, Northampton, Massachusetts.

Page 4
Self-Portrait, 1942. Oil on canvas, 24 × 16⅞" (61 × 43 cm). Smith College Museum of Art, Northampton, Massachusetts. Gift of Irene Rich Clifford.

Page 5
The Making of a Fresco, Showing the Building of a City (detail), April–June 1931. Fresco, 18'7⅝ × 32'6⅛" (5.68 × 9.91 m). San Francisco Art Institute, San Francisco, California.

Page 6
Tlatilco figurines, Anahuacalli. Photograph by Deborah Nagao, courtesy the author.

Page 7
Calaveras in Rivera's studio, Anahuacalli. Photograph by Deborah Nagao, courtesy the author.

Page 9
Day of the Dead—City Fiesta, 1923–24. Fresco, 13'8⅛ × 12'3⅝" (4.17 × 3.75 m). Court of Fiestas, Ministry of Public Education, Mexico City, Mexico (photo © Bob Schalwijk, courtesy Art Resource).

Page 10
Sleeping Woman, 1921. Crayon, 24⅝ × 18½" (62.7 × 46.9 cm). Fogg Art Museum, Harvard University Art Museums, Cambridge, Massachussetts. Bequest of Meta and Paul J. Sachs.

Page 12
Dance in Tehuantepec, 1931. Oil on canvas, 6'6⅜ × 63¾" (199 × 162 cm). Collection IBM Corporation, Armonk, New York.

Page 13
Zapatista Landscape (The Guerilla), 1915. Oil on canvas, 56¼ × 48⅜" (143.8 × 123.2 cm). National Museum of Art, Mexico City, Mexico (photo courtesy Art Resource).

Page 15
Leaving the Mine, 1923. Fresco, 15'8¼ × 7'1⅝" (4.78 × 2.15 m). Court of Labor, Ministry of Public Education, Mexico City, Mexico (photo © Bob Schalwijk, courtesy Art Resource).

Page 16
Distributing Arms, 1928. Fresco, 8'4¾ × 11'9" (2.56 × 3.58 m). Ministry of Public Education, Mexico City, Mexico (photo © Dirk Bakker).

Page 17
Diego Rivera and Frida Kahlo, c. 1940. Photograph by Nicholas Murray. International Museum of Photography at George Eastman House, Rochester, New York.

Page 18
The Paradise of Tlaloc, c. 300–600. Fresco. Teotihuacán, Mexico (photo © Jeffrey J. Foxx).

Pages 20–21
View of chapel showing *The Liberated Earth with Natural Forces Controlled by Man,* 1926–27. Fresco, 22'8½ × 19'7½" (6.92 × 5.98 m). Chapel, Autonomous University of Chapingo (photo © Dirk Bakker).

Page 21
Blood of the Revolutionary Martyrs Fertilizing the Earth, 1926–27. Fresco, 8' × 16'1¼" (2.44 × 4.91 m). Chapel, Autonomous University of Chapingo (photo © Dirk Bakker).

Pages 22–23
Sketch for The History of Mexico, central wall, National Palace, 1925. Museum of Technology, Mexico City. (photo © Bob Schalwijk, courtesy Art Resource).

Page 24
Top: *Battle of the Aztecs and Spaniards* (detail), also known as *The Conquest,* 1930–31. Fresco, approx. 14'3¼ × 7'5" (4.35 × 2.26 m). Palace of Cortés, Cuernavaca, Mexico (photo courtesy Art Resource).
Bottom: Ritual combat between eagle knight and prisoner. From the Florentine Codex. Biblioteca Medicea Laurenziana, Florence, Italy.

Page 25
The Aztec World, also known as *Before the Conquest,* 1929. Fresco, 24'6⅞ × 29'½" (7.49 × 8.85 m). National Palace, Mexico City, Mexico (photo © Bob Schalwijk, courtesy Art Resource).

Page 26
The founding of Tenochtitlán, from the Codex Tovar.

Page 27
From the Conquest to 1930 (detail), 1929–30. Fresco. National Palace, Mexico City, Mexico (photo courtesy Art Resource).

Page 28
Study for the *Popul Vuh,* c. 1931.

Page 29
Agrarian Leader Zapata, 1931. Fresco, 7'9¾ × 6'2" (2.38 × 1.88 m). The Museum of Modern Art, New York, Abby Aldrich Rockefeller Fund.

Page 30
Atlantean Warriors, Toltec, 1000–1200. Stone, height approx. 15' (4.57 m). Tula, Hidalgo, Mexico (photo © Jeffrey J. Foxx).

Page 31
Detroit Industry, North Wall, 1932–33. Fresco, 17'8½ × 45' (5.40 × 13.72 m). Detroit Institute of Arts, Detroit, Michigan. Founders Society Purchase, Edsel B. Ford Fund, and Gift of Edsel B. Ford (photo © Detroit Institute of Arts).

Page 33
Flower Day, 1925. Encaustic on canvas, 58 × 47½" (147.4 × 120.6 cm). Los Angeles County Fund, Los Angeles County Museum of Art, Los Angeles, California.

Page 34
Untitled (market scene), 1931.

Page 35
Goddess with tassled headdress, Aztec, c. 1350–1521. Basalt, height 11¾" (29.8 cm). Museum of Ethnology, Basel, Switzerland (photo by Peter Horner).

Pages 36–37
Exterior pool showing *The Rain God, Tlaloc,* 1951. Stone mosaic. Lerma Waterworks, Mexico City, Mexico (photo © Dirk Bakker).

Page 38
Ruins of Mexican City of Teotihuacán which flourished c. 300 B.C.–900 A.D. Photo courtesy the Granger Collection.

Page 39
Top: Exterior of Anahuacalli. Photograph by Deborah Nagao, courtesy the author.
Bottom: Interior of Anahuacalli. Photograph by Deborah Nagao, courtesy the author.

Pages 40–41
Dream of a Sunday Afternoon in the Alameda (detail), 1947–48. Fresco, 15' × 49'2½" (4.8 × 15 m). Diego Rivera Mural Museum (formerly at Hotel del Prado), Mexico City, Mexico (photo © Dirk Bakker).

Page 43
Top: *Jaguar Figurine with Wheels,* Nopiloa, c. 300–900. Terra-cotta, length 7⅛" (18.1 cm). Anthropology Museum, Veracruzana University, Jalapa, Mexico (photo © Jeffrey J. Foxx).
Bottom: *Burden Bearer,* Jalisco, c. 250 B.C.–A.D. 250. Terra-cotta. Diego Rivera Museum, Mexico City, Mexico (photo © Jeffrey J. Foxx).

Pages 44–45
The Great City of Tenochtitlán, 1945. Fresco, 16'1¾ × 31'10¼" (4.92 × 9.71 m). Patio Corridor, National Palace, Mexico City, Mexico (photo © Bob Schalwijk, courtesy Art Resource).

Page 46
Untitled, 1931.

Page 48
The Flower Carrier, 1935. Oil and tempera on masonite, 48 × 47¾" (121.9 × 121.3 cm). San Francisco Museum of Modern Art, Albert M. Bender Collection. Gift of Albert M. Bender in memory of Caroline Walter.

Page 63
The Rivera residence and studio in San Angel. Photo courtesy Bertram D. Wolfe Collection, Hoover Institution Archives, Stanford University, Stanford, California.

For my daughter, Miranda

First published in the United States of America in 1994 by
Rizzoli International Publications, Inc.
300 Park Avenue South
New York, New York 10010

Library of Congress Cataloging-in-Publication Data

Braun, Barbara, 1939–
    A Weekend With Diego Rivera / by Barbara Braun
        p. cm.
    ISBN 0-8478-1749-0
    1. Rivera, Diego, 1886–1957—Juvenile literature. 2. Artists—
Mexico—Biography—Juvenile literature. [1. Rivera, Diego,
1886–1957. 2. Artists.] I. Rivera, Diego, 1886–1957. II. Title.
N6559.R58B73 1994
759.972—dc20   93-38905
[B]   CIP
                                                    AC

Design by Mary McBride
Editors: Lois Brown
          David Brown

Printed in Hong Kong